LITTLE WORMS THAT EAT

THE APPLE

Building The Church Without Crises

Samuel Johnson

LITTLE WORMS THAT EAT

THE APPLE

TABLE OF CONTENT

Chapter one

The true concept of Christian and the calling 23

- Calling in Christianity
- The Gift and Calling
- Workers and Function of the Office
- Selection into Office

Chapter two

The leadership in the church 46

- What is leadership?
- Leaders and Office
- Purpose driven Leadership

Chapter three

The worm in the apple – The falsified nuggets that corrupt the beauty of the church and purpose..........................64

- Discipleship of Members

Acknowledgment

My profound appreciation is given to Almighty God for the grace to successfully, bring this work to your reach.

I will not fail to appreciate my wife, Ronke, my beloved Covenant and Faithful for their understanding during the process of completion.

I also give recognition to friends in ministry for all their contributions to the completion of this work. I pray that my Father in Heaven will greatly reward you abundantly.

It is my earnest prayer that
God Almighty will grant you
more grace till you bear more
good fruits to this kingdom.

Dedication

This work is dedicated to all church leaders who seek effective ministry in our challenging age.

Preface

In my earnest observation, the church is facing several challenges that have bereaved so many disciples' zeal and faith. However, it will be considered appropriate searching through the time and commending the right approach to things that corrupt our effort.

Apple is bigger than the worm; yet the little worm is very disastrous to apple. If worm is not fetched out of apple, then, the apple's beauty and value will be lost. Let us compare what this is to the local church. Negligence to tackle this little fact will give enough rooms for good visions in local ministries and churches to die or become unproductive.

Certainly, this work is built on the inspiration of the Holy Spirit. After a careful study on local churches and their inability to effect desired change in their vision and mission. A practical evaluation was conducted with some local churches and their workers, it became necessary to bring to the general church, what each leader and church should keep to in other to secure effectiveness of purpose and service.

However, I am setting a practical challenge. I am convinced it will give a positive change. If you will admit what is discussed in this work with humbleness of mind and pursue working out purpose, you will have tangible effective operation with yielding fruit.

This work is not an exhaustive work to solve all crises in local church; rather, it will help you the leader to lay a good foundation that will reduce crises to a controllable rate. Therefore, I encourage that you read this work prayerfully and put in effort to adapt to the area that needs change as you will be realizing them.

It is my earnest prayer that God Almighty will grant you more grace till you bear more good fruits to this kingdom.

Samuel Johnson
The Author

Foreword

*L*ittle Worms That Eats the Apple is structured material for leaders (at all level) and for reader that feels he has a "Calling of God" with a passion in his life right from birth. Leaders who have the love to win souls for God's with every role given to play in a church at any given opportunity as if life depends upon it.

Before reading this book, I have lived the experience, the confusion from misinterpretation of boundaries towards position on leadership and authority. I am grateful that this book helped me to understand that every single role played in the church has a vital impact to one's life, and to the body of Christ as stated in chapter 2: "The perfection of the body of Christ lies on the effective commitment from different existing organs in the body." This is a must acquire understanding that every leader within the church should have. Now I, professionally have better understanding along with the awakening spirit that bears witness to the word of God Almighty and to eliminate uncalled dogma that creates a platform of confusion to the younger leaders that are coming up for Christ.

Little Worms That Eats the Apple has given me insights on orderliness towards evidence of soundness. Soundness that leads to the ability to lead and act of guidance, of which I have acknowledged as person of influence to get things done. The next insight is being a big picture thinker, to get people excited to where they are going and how to get there. I express how precious it is to believe the best in people by giving them benefit of doubts; gather all facts before drawing to conclusion on things. Another is about seeing oneself with consistent credibility and the skill of a teacher as well as a mentor. This has given me the platform to build others to grow through delegations; that shows a result of being responsible to any leadership opportunity that one comes across.

This book has also enlightened me in the area of master delegations to where one learns from mistakes and work experience. Team player is another skill that I have acquired to work with others. This helps me to work confidently with whosoever that I came across. Ethic and integrity are major for me both in business and otherwise, it is a mandate to practice with trust to demonstrate the leadership in the church. Accounting with transparent practices also enrich the livelihood of leadership. The code of conduct manages the practical aspect of organizational integrity. The list is endless. Wisdom here has no price tag but creates an impressive milestone to life values in local churches of today.

I personally thank the Lord today for Johnson, S. (Author), *Little Worm That Eats the Apple* to allow himself to be inspired by the Holy Spirit. Samuel Johnson has been the one that was able to pull me out from my self-destruction due to so many heartaches from church leaders, men and women of God.

Elizabeth Jack

Introduction

*"And thou shalt **teach** them **ordinances** and **laws,** and shalt **shew** them the **way** wherein they must **walk,** and the **work** that they must **do.** Moreover thou shalt **provide** out of all the people **able men**, such as fear God, men of truth, hating covetousness; and place such over them,…And let them judge the people at all seasons:…If thou shalt do this thing, and God command thee so, then thou shalt be able to endure, and all this people shall also go to their place in peace…"* Exodus 18: 20-23 (emphases added)

Building the church without crises is building church in accordance with God's purpose and will. Knowing the will of God and pursuing God's mandate is working in purpose and plan. Will a church grow with glory and power; it is a church that follows biblical principles; and constantly, pursuing and balancing their decisions with biblical standard.

We are faced with the challenge of bringing the church of God into maturity. We have this mandate from God, to feed the church with right food; nurture them to grow healthier; helping them to become strong and useful like us. Here is what Paul said to the church in Colossi; *"Him we preach and proclaim, warning and admonishing everyone and instructing everyone in all wisdom (comprehensive insight into the ways and purposes of God), that we may present every person mature (full-grown, fully initiated, complete, and perfect) in Christ (the Anointed One).* Colossians 1: 28 (AMP.)

The Lord is willing to see us perform our responsibilities. We are given a privilege to serve. We are working in God's kingdom, preparing the bride (church) for the groom, Jesus Christ our Lord. It will be a beautiful and glorious thing standing before the Father who will be pleased with what we have done. Alternatively, if we fail to keep the house of God in order; *'leading the church in biblical principles, show them the way wherein they must walk, and the work that they must do. More so entrusting office (port-folio) to able men who will judge God's people in righteousness, truth, hating covetousness, never exalt themselves above the people but humbly lead them to God in maturity;'* you can guess what it will be like when our time is up.

Let us be prepared to take a bold step to change things that were wrongly placed and give the Holy Spirit the chance to set the church in the manner the Father our Maker wants. Let us allow our self-pride to go; seek for the JOY of the Father our Maker. This is where our obedience for reward lies and we will get it. Our salvation is precious, and we have to work it out by all means while on earth. This is a golden privilege; indeed, it is high calling from the Almighty God.

MAKE YOUR NOTE

CHAPTER ONE

A Christian is a precious earthen vessel that carries the heavenly treasure in earth. The sacredness of this mystery is revealed daily by constant senses to the things within and outside the church in events that happened in life. This work will be of greater effect to the Christian within the local church and the affair will be the concern. Even though the term Christian is a very familiar word, we will consider it for better understanding on what we will be discussing.

Who is a Christian?

The church is made up of Christian. W. T. P Wolston says, in his book 'handful of purpose', "The church of God is composed of those who have been redeemed by Christ, been washed in His blood, born of the spirit, possess a new nature, are sealed by the Holy Spirit, and are then, baptized into one body."

According to W. A. Criswell, "A New Testament church of the Lord Jesus Christ is a local body of baptized believers who are associated by covenant in the faith and fellowship of the gospel, observing the two ordinances of Christ, committed to His teachings, exercising the gifts, rights, and privileges invested in them by His word, and seeking to extend the gospel to the ends of the earth." Criswell's guidebook for Pastors.

A Christian in this regards is not he that goes to church; or is one that has his name in church register, paying tithes and offering to the church; rather, is one whose life is evident of his confession of faith. Furthermore, he is one who speaks or shares what he believes and does what he wants others to do, giving his obeisance to God only.

So, the church organization is a unified entity of persons with cooperate purpose and focus. By the above definition, it is certain that, the man who is called the Christian is one who is transformed from the old nature to a new nature, covenanted with a precious blood and his state of person is witness by the Holy Spirit. What a beautiful man in a glorious entity.

Man responds to the invitation of God. He accepts the call willingly and he is integrated into one body and equipped for a unique purpose. He is called a Christian because he believes in Christ, His visions and His mission.

Calling in Christianity

Many people misrepresent the term Christianity as religion. Christianity is not religion. It is a lifestyle of the people who follow the Savior of man, Jesus the Christ. It has to do with acceptance of purpose and truth from God. It is evidence of the response to ultimate invitation from the Maker –

God Almighty.

We must take note here that the Christian concept of the *'call'* does have the basic elements of Attraction of Attention, a Response that could be positive or negative. Important of all is that the call of God is on purpose. God does not call a man without a purpose but for him to meet a specific purpose.

Every Christian is called. But there are different dimensions of call. All are called unto repentance. Everyone is daily responding to call by God. It could be negative response or positive response. Everything around us is invitation to God. Events that take place within the immediate and remote environment are communicating the reality and the calling of God to humanity. God wants us to accept Him as the creator of all things; and to give Him the due devotion by our positive response to Him.

'They (the unbelievers in the world) know the truth about God because he has made it obvious to them. For ever since the world was created, people have seen the earth and sky. Through everything God made, they can clearly see his invisible qualities – his eternal power and divine nature. So, they have no excuse for not knowing God.' Romans1:19-20. (NLT) emphases added.

In the gospel of John 3: 16; God gave opportunity inviting all that is willing to come to repentance.

'For God so loved the world, that he gave His only begotten Son, that whosoever believeth in him should not perish, but have everlasting life.'

And to the church that is made up of Christians (those who have received the called unto repentance) are **called unto service**. The call of the church is all positive response. As Christians, we are without excuse if denying the call unto service.

Here every Christian progress from the mere foundation of salvation and repentance to a higher ground of effective service in the body of Christ. Paul writing to the body of Christ in Ephesians 4:1 declares:

'I, therefore, the prisoner of the Lord, beseech you to walk worthy of the calling with which you were called.' (NKJV)

It is clear that every believer has a vocation (a calling) in the body to fulfill. Also, the Apostle again declares the state of the believer in the call to service. *'For I say, through the grace given to me, to everyone who is among you, not to think of himself more highly than he ought to think, but to think soberly, as God has dealt to each one a measure of faith.'* Romans 12: 3 (NKJV)

The scripture says everyone is given

grace according to the measure of faith. Not some, but every believer. We are composite of gifts. Great is the treasure that we carry. Everyone is call into service as a believer. You are already called; you have something within you designed by God for His purpose. You are to present yourself suitable for the master's use. Covert the higher place of honor by valuing the gift of God in your life. Give all diligent to whatever is laid in your hand. Do it as unto God who gave you what you have and made you who you are. *'But in a great house there are not only vessels of gold and of silver, but also of wood and of earth; and some to honor, and some to dishonor.'* 2Timothy 2: 20.

More so, there are others who are called into special called. At special call, one is call into higher commitment. This is the stage of call where God from the second stage of commitment and service selects a few or some into a higher commitment and service. This is the five-fold ministry classified as priestly office.

'And he gave some, apostles; and some, prophets; and some, evangelists; and some, pastors and teachers.' Ephesians 4:11

A healthy congregation is that with five-fold ministry operational. It is very important, because each of this office is specifically designed to meet the need in the body of Christ – church. Where this is not cultivated, then the church is likely experiencing spiritual leanness. Read 1Corinthians 12. Ephesian 4: 12,13.

In the above three sectors of calling, all are controlled under divine purpose. Therefore, anyone that responds positively to call is response to purpose. Similarly, when one responds negatively to divine call absolutely, he simply withdraws from completing the purpose of existence.

God laid His hand upon us with divine purpose. Our call unto God is call unto service. It therefore means that to every, everyone that answer the call have in him the ability to meet up what he was called to do. Let us clarify this concept. Your answer to call is response to the caller and is important and purposeful; and him that answered the call is important and useful to the caller. Whatever you are, be known you have gift and virtue that is very important.

There are certain acts of calling that operate in the local churches. And we will look into it briefly to draw out basic understanding that will help both the local church head and leaders within any local assembly to reposition their vision and mission mandate.

Appointment

Several ministries and even secular organization suffer the setback whenever the true concept on 'appointment' is misappropriated. Although this term is often used to express circumference of time yet, it requires more delicate application mostly when it is used within the church administrative context. Let us see what appointment should be considered in our local assemblies.

The concept here implies the act of making or setting a place or position to function. When one receives appointment, he is called into service. He is assigned, designated, or set apart by authority. He receives a place that defines what he has to share with others effectively; He releases into the body of Christ the riches of his faith in Christ. In other word, when we are appointed or appoint someone, it means that we or the person have a specific gift or ability to work out the given need in the local church, the body of Christ.

Office

The term office from the Latin word, *'officium'* means 'doing work'. In this concept, it denotes 'acting' or 'function'. It means that believers either ecclesiastical (believers) call or special call are called and appointed into a given place of work or duty. Take note, you are not given title rather you are given duty to perform.

What does acting *implies?*

To act implies that one is exerting ideas and abilities together towards a known and decisive result. You are acting upon a thing or event to gain the end point. The office in the church is given for a specify direction of ideas and abilities to fulfill a purpose.

Let head of local churches and fellowship centers give this knowledge to the people that they have been called into service. Let the people know what they are called in to do. The work or ministry should be taught effectively.

Several training should be conducted intensively to secure the maximum performance of the worker in a given office. I further suggest that the training should be a fundamental duty. Training should be given to the general congregation. When your congregation is undergoing constant training, you are guaranteed to have sound formative service. Make training a tradition in your congregation. It will help you congregation become 'your' vision oriented. It will give them sense of unity of faith and purpose.

The Gift and Calling

Christians are gifted individuals that occupy the house of God. They have several abilities to serve efficiently in their given area of their calling. The Holy Spirit dwells in us with power. He strengthens us, gives us enablement so that we can understand the things in God's house and do them orderly. In Acts 1:8, Jesus said, *"But ye shall receive power when the Holy Spirit is come upon you…"* The power received by Christian is gift from God. The gift is for witnessing – *perfecting the saints, the work of ministry, and the edifying of the body.* Ephesians 4:12.

"As every man hath received the gift, even so minister the same one to another, as good stewards of the manifold grace of God." 1Peter 4:10

The Holy Spirit is the Enabler. He gives strength to your natural abilities you were born with. Listen, God prepared you right from your mother's womb. He made you complete with substance that are unique. Every man is born with greatness. The Holy Spirit gives attention to this blessing. In this regards you are positioned by God in the right place to unveil your full potentials. Take note, your efficiency is only known in every attempt to bring needs or challenges under your control. The more you get involve with the activities in your area of calling or appointment, the more the Holy Spirit gives you grace for effectiveness and efficiency. He works perfectly with those who rely on Him.

"…For He lives with you and will be in you…" John14:17 (NIV).

As Christian, you are to take responsibility in the church. Get involved in the ministry that you see is in need of attention. Put the best in you, that is the development of your abilities. You will not know how efficient you are until you take responsibility. The best in you is sharpened through responsibility. Never shy away. Never say you are not recognized. Your leader may not know what your natural endowment is. You need to introduce your abilities. Be participant and not spectator. It is your Father's house. The church needs your positive contribution to accomplish its task on earth.

Everyone that receives and responds to ecclesiastical calling is coming into fulfilling God's intent and purpose. When he called us into office to serve, He equally gives us the required gift that will help us discharge the service efficiently.

Workers and Function of the Office

It will be wise if the church members will recognize that if we desire an office without discerning the natural talent and gift that is given to us, we will be disappointed to know that, we only occupy space, and have no impact to the church and lives. We should not quest for place of promotion or honor in the church, rather, the place where we can effectively serve the Lord.

Every man is useful in the house of the Lord. To each one is given gift according to purpose. Passion for a position should be followed by purpose and gift. God told Jeremiah the reason why he was chosen undermining his age and his supposed inability.

'Before I formed thee in the belly, I knew thee; and before thou camest forth out of the womb I sanctified thee, and I ordained thee a prophet unto the nations. Then said I, Ah, Lord GOD! Behold, I cannot speak for I am a child. But the LORD said unto me, say not, I am a child: for thou shalt go to all that I shall send thee, and whatsoever I command thee thou shalt speak.' Jeremiah1: 5 – 7.

Functioning Is Impacting

Effective church growth and crises control is the spirit of impact. Such church with these concepts is one that shapes it abilities to fulfill the vision and to accomplish its mission. Getting committed to right things within the need-system of your local church is removing the itching factor that wars against the success of the congregation. The church office is emerging as a result of certain lack that the church is growing into. Let this be noted, no office exists for decoration. Each of it is an opportunity given *'that the man of God may be perfect, thoroughly furnished unto all good works.'* 2Timothy 3:17.

Becoming the leader church needs is God's purpose focus oriented. We have to see what we have to do at a given time, as what God grant us to fulfill at this age. However, the impact we pursue to deliver in God fearing Spirit and leadership is worth the measure of growth we attend in Christ.

This is the spirit of maturity. The worker in the church that is growing in this passion is certainly going to make laudable impact. And if you as a head in your ministry and church have people operating with this concept, mutuality of faith will grow. Crises will be under effective control.

Selection into Office
The selection into office is the

most problematic aspect in the church. And it is a welcome issue that requires the attention of the church as a whole. The selection into the office should be viewed with dependence on the Holy Spirit. The people's faith should be considered, and fervency should be their quality plus.

Paul in his epistle to Timothy forewarned that nominating persons into office should not be done by sentiment. Neither should one whose faith has not been certified and much room given to be acclimatized clarify into office.

'…Not a novice, lest being lifted up with pride he falls into the condemnation of the devil. Moreover, he must have a good report of them which are without; lest he fall into reproach and the snare of the devil.' 1 Timothy 3: 6-7.

In Acts of the Apostles, Peter and other apostles called on the congregation to choose among them men filled with the Holy Spirit and of good report; that they will authorize them to oversee the affair of the table while they continue in the teaching of the word and the preaching of the gospel.

'Wherefore, brethren, look ye out among you seven men of honest report, full of the Holy Ghost and wisdom, whom we may appoint over this business.' Acts 6: 3.

They had one thing in mind, and that is, the selecting individuals for the position of service must be men of *good report, full of the Holy Spirit* and *wisdom.* This is because they are taking over authority to function in the assembly of people with common belief and purpose. These people are spiritually elected by God for His kingdom.

More so, the church leaders should have this in mind that selecting anyone into an office is assigning one with authority to carry out the assigned duty. Therefore, the effect of the authority will produce the fruit of the knowledge of what the individual has. Let it be a mandate that you spend quality time to build the people in the Church; to know what calling God has called them into and the necessity to be effective on the vocation they are called into.

"I, therefore, the prisoner of the LORD, beseech you that ye walk worthy of the vocation wherewith ye are called." Ephesians 4: 1.

Four basic biblical principles to selection.

The following biblical principles for selection into office can be of greater help to assist your leadership ministry effective.

1. *He must have the testimony of his salvation.*
2. *He must be filled with the Holy Spirit*
3. *He must have a good report within and outside the church*
4. *He must be apt to teaching.*

The most important thing is that the church-leader should grow the attitude of total dependence on the Holy Spirit for proper selection, if you take a look at Gideon, Judge7:7; God made a proper selection on those who are competent to face the reality of the calling and will carry their cross without failing. The leadership traits should never be overlooked before selecting them for office appointment. The Apostles said to the people, select from among you men of honest report, full of the Holy Spirit and wisdom. Acts 6: 3.

See appendix for details.

MAKE YOUR NOTE

CHAPTER TWO

THE LEADERSHIP IN THE CHURCH

The most unique organism that God ever called into existence is the church – the body of Christ. The church is a multi-functional organism that operates with capable unique talents and gifts with the ultimate purpose of manifesting the reality of God and Jesus Christ and His tangible Glory that is eternal.

It is an organism with eternal structure. Not with materials made by man. Rather, it is that whose foundation, that is the chief corner stone, we the living stone are build (structure) upon. With such a unique mastered formation, the operation of the church becomes unique in its nature. Certainly, the church is functional in existence and liable to the impartation of life to people within and abroad.

The church is an organism with eternal structure. Therefore, her structure should be orderly structured. What do I mean? Pauline anatomy illustrates the efficiency the church can affect in any part of the world. This is true, each members of the body are designed to function in optimum capacity. Whenever any person (biological system) givens out or is perform at full capacity we conclude it to be good. Likewise, it is in the body of Christ – the church. The body grows into macro-functional body. The members are working together; discharging their functions effectively, to make the gathered ones unique in person and perfect in nature unto God. This is beautiful.

It is the human instrument that is to be placed orderly for effective operation and functioning of God's purposes. The church foundation is not in accordance with human wisdom; rather, this is a body whose foundation is laid in Christ in accordance with the wisdom of God the Almighty. It is an institution that is established by the principles ordained by God himself.

Therefore, to every function that the church is designed to carry out should be based on the objective of fulfilling the ultimate purpose and will of the Father.

Orderliness is the evidence of soundness of mind.
1 Corinthians 14:40, Paul concluded his first letter analysis on the *functioning-anatomy* this way.

"Let all things be done decently and in order."

Jesus requires the human instrument for effective administration of things that are necessary for the body, which is on earth. In the time of Moses, the father in-law Jethro being inspired by God, advised him on how to appoint people into leadership office and delegate works to them. In the New Testament writing Paul an apostle of our Lord Jesus Christ under the inspiration of the Holy Spirit gave a clearer picture on the church leaders and their responsibilities.

"…That you should set in order the things that are lacking…" Titus 1: 5. (NKJV)

"…For the equipping of the saints for the work of ministry, for the edifying of the body of Christ." Ephesians 4:11,12.

The perfection of the body of Christ lies on the effective commitment from different existing organs in the body. When the people know what is required of them; and the senses of duties are made close to their accessibility. Then the church will experience the awakening of sustained growth.

The comrade of the kingdom building is the workers in the church. It is imperative that we give careful evaluation to the existing organs of leadership in the church. Careful observation drew our attention to the plight that is robbing the church. The whole functioning organs need to be bred together. That is, the understanding of the individual organ of administration will uniquely produce the soundness of their respective part and will in turn beautify the whole system of the church. In a situation that it is neglected, the church will suffer crises such as; Church breaking, reduction of membership attendance, non-participatory attitude on social and spiritual needs of the members and church in general, non-cordial respect for one another, and many unwelcome immoral traits.

Who is a leader?

It will be satisfactory to build on a practical definition that will help sensitize the communal issues that decay the effort of leadership within the church.

'A leader is one who leads others.'

To lead could mean, 'to guard and guide one into purpose'. To redefine it; *'a leader is one who guards and guides one into purpose'.* That is, he guards – protects the people from losing value, prevent them from been distracted by wrong ideas, controls them to gain understanding; guides – shows or influences them the way to achieve it, helping them learn more of what they want to achieve, and motivate them to continue till they accomplish the purpose.

A leader can also be seen as *'one who guides and develops the activities and abilities of others.*

What Is Leadership?

Leadership will be considered as the special ability *'to set goals in accordance with God's purposes for the future and to communicate those goals to others in such a way that they voluntarily and harmoniously work together to accomplish the goals for the glory of God.'*

Leadership function is the activities

done by a leader to influence the people's thinking, behavior personally or professionally. Anyone in the leadership position should be able to manifest leadership function.

- Such a leader should have a 'strong desire' to persuade others to achieve biblical objectives.
- Such should have great knowledge on where he is going and seeing others following him.
- Such should have pleasure in leading, inspiring, and motivating others to do the Lord's work.
- Such should build strong will to influence others to accomplish tasks and biblical purposes.
- Such should be master and complaint with God's word and will to edifying and perfecting others belief.

Therefore, I assumed leadership to be:

1. **An inspiration:** It has to do with what one can see with his mental sight before communicating to others. If he

has not such ability then, he has nothing to show or influence the people with.

2. **Nature that exists within:** True leadership is natural life one live. It has no *pseudo* manner. It is the reaction of your nature that is what your person is. You are directly responsible to your action. Your action is a product of internal reality of your heart. Leadership comes from the heart.

3. **Quality of life:** It can be regarded as characteristics of individual. Effective leadership begins with leading your attitude. How you feel, think and act is leadership.

4. **Purpose oriented:** Leadership is centered on purpose. And without purpose there is no reason for leading people. Purpose is what birth leading.

5. **Result affair:** Leadership is an act that is performed by individual with sole aim of fulfilling or satisfying the drive within. Leadership is said to be efficient only when results are seen.

6. Relationship: The act of leading is two ways affair. Every leader needs people to lead. The same people are leaders at a given capacity. You have to create reciprocating atmosphere to enable you share and guard them into your vision and purpose. Without leadership you cannot nurture God's people. Because you have to love them and show the love you have for them with evident. Love is demonstration. and not confession

Leaders and Office

All organs in the body of Christ are taken care by one that is either called or appointed to meet the need and vacancy that is suddenly or gradually awakening the sustaining growth of the church. The need and vacancy in the local church is significant change for growth. For example, when your congregation numerical growth is unstable; inconsistence in members' attitude to meet in church activities; it is indication that visitation ministry is needed or if acknowledged, then, be empowered. Therefore, people would be called to fill in the vacancy. Whenever there is called for people to positively respond, it means that there is a need for someone to function or do the work required. Furthermore, it is call for one to put in his knowledge and abilities to fulfill demand in the ministry.

The vacancy is caused by emergence of growth. The growth is not numerical growth only, but both spiritual and natural ability. You have to take every opportunity that exists to build yourself and develop others. Its leadership is responsibility. It is to be exercised with intention to fulfill the purpose of its existence.

The leader should not be put off from this knowledge; that he is timely placed in a given office of his appointment or calling, to meet with the desire and need of the people he is leading. This is in line with the divine sovereignty of God to actualize his purpose with everyone he chooses. Every leader is very important as the office: because we are coming together to make the body of Christ perfect and unique in nature. Therefore, the office is essential as it is thus strengthening and edifies the body. The church is the body of Christ. To every office is given gift that is appropriate to the necessity of the office. It could be said that every leader is equipped in abundance as required in his given office of service.

"…to each according to his own ability…" Matthew 25: 15.
"And the grace of our Lord was exceeding abundant…" 1Timothy 1: 14

The pastor, elder, deacon, usher and others have the measure of faith that will make them function well. But it will be unhealthy if the measure of faith in the life of individual is not discerned before appointment into office. Every believer has a starting point in faith. Never over-faith the ability within the people you appointed. Talents and gifts grow in process and not automatic. Be patient with the members, to discover and be convinced that the measure of work allotted can be carried out without creating crises to other functioning ministries.

Purpose Driven Leadership

Christ instructed us to seek the kingdom of God first; invariably, the leader's first priority and ultimate drive is to manifest the reality of the kingdom. As a leader, you are directed to operate or function according to the kingdom principles.

In the great commission, the Lord Jesus commanded that we should make the people who believe the gospel his disciples. Paul in his letter to the church in Ephesus said that the disciples are fellow citizens of the kingdom. So, the church is the gathering of the citizens. Thereby, their purpose is unique and directed with one goal in life. Therefore, our leadership function should be designed to foster this great purpose.

Myles Munroe in his book, 'Becoming a leader' said; *"Leadership is impossible without a guiding vision and a purpose that generates passion for accomplishment."* In his concept, vision is what guide in your purpose and while your understanding on your purpose of existence gives birth or generates passion.

Purpose and Passion

Understanding the purpose in life and the salvation that each one of us have in Christ will generate the passion for leadership. To be called into an office and position is not religious celebrity rather it is responsibility given to be carried out.

You can't be committed to what you don't know anything about. And it is the volume of knowledge you have over a thing that will position your interest, which births strong zeal that drives you to success.

A worker is called into an office with the purpose to help others (members of local assembly and the body of Christ in general) satisfy their passion for Christ. The duty of the church worker within the church will be to make the people of the same worship center become fruitful to God. But when the primary objective of calling one into office by appointment is neglected or less attention is given; then, the growth of the local assembly will suffer setback. More so, the spiritual stand of the individual members will wax cold. Heads, founders and general overseers of local church must take a break and re-examine their drive towards various appointment they have and those placed. Let us come to this understanding: 'our best should be tailored with our ability to guide and guard emerging leaders in our local congregation to purpose fulfillment'.

This is very important, your vision and set goal lie linearly by what commitment you have towards the quality of person you call into office. Your leadership should maintain the focus to influence the people called into position to become the very best of their abilities in life in the very vision that you have shared with them. At this point, there is bound to be agreement and sustainable unity in love and value within the local church.

Your local congregation would stand a better future when the people have similar mind-set with their leader. And the possibilities to venture on new development within the local church will not be the thing of the head of the local church; rather, it will be all people embraced project. How beautiful would that look like?

Therefore, the leadership should eradicate all trace of worms that easily devalue the strength of vision. Take a giant stand to embrace any change this work is about to call for in your local church operation. Take note, a parachute is at its best when it is opened.

MAKE YOUR NOTE

CHAPTER THREE

Disturbances in new era church grow alarmingly in this generation because basic things that church leaders should have put in place is not considered necessary to follow. These grow gradually and steadily and become influencing structure in the body of Christ. Even when we are bordered with the dimension in which crises are affecting the church, yet we never seek diligently the right way to control the crises.

Working in the church setting is one of the most challenging tasks. This is so, because the church itself is the gathering of different kind of background of people cutting across age, social status, tribes, profession and temperament and destiny of purpose. In some community, you have different ethnicities. Then one should embrace the fact that many of the converts are still struggling to overcome culture bias and personality challenges. These and other things that are not observed become the strength that opposes the smooth growth of the vision of the church.

Do not forget, why leadership occur is the result of needs to guide and guard. Then, one that is coming into this responsibility should have been clarified the essence of his coming into the leading or have sense of direction so as to direct those entrusted into his hand. Therefore, workers and leaders need to consider some of these issues that will be considered here and re-examine their performances and give room for change where necessary.

Office Awareness

To be informed is to be in the form for effectiveness. The leader whose duty is not understood is bound to make several mistakes. This is as the result of his state of awareness. He can perform his function effectively only on what he knows; and can lead on what he knows only.

Several leaders (church heads) have played low on the necessity to broaden the understanding of the workers in the church. This neglected exercise stands as exigency to the modern church in this part of the world. The resent exercise conducted shows that about 85% of the entire church worker do not know what the task and purpose is in the distinguish ministries of the church.

A healthy growing church should not be measured in the miraculous account on event that occurs in the church. Rather, it should be considered on the maturity of the ministries being able to manage the crises either active or remote in respective local church (congregation).

The apostle Paul in his analyses on the anatomy of the church sequentially shows the usefulness of all organs that constitute the body. Side by side, explaining the structure of the church, even that which is spiritual and that which is physical, said, is dependable and can only be useful when each other recognizes the importance of the others.

'But now God has set the members, each one of them, in the body just as He pleased. And if they were all one member, where would the body be? But now indeed there are many members, yet one body…And those members of the body which we think to be less honorable, on these we bestow greater honor; and our unpresentable parts have greater modesty, but our presentable parts have no need. But God composed the body, having given greater honor to that part which lacks it, that there should be no schism in the body, but that the members should have the same care for one another…Now you are the body of Christ, and members individual…' 1 Corinthians 12:12-31. (NKJV)
"…let all things be done decently and in order." 1Corinthians 14:40.

To further amplify the concept of the context. It will be fair to apply this on our porosity to envisage the result when workers in the church are appointed in offices without adequate training to measure the challenges that the church is facing. The training concept should have been cultivated to help produce effective workers that will carry the vision and burden of the church to the fulfillment of God's purpose and plan.

It will be wise to dislodge our mind on often measuring success on numerical growth in the church. Practically Mathew 28:20; emphasizes the growth dimension, '…*teaching them to observe all things...*' the compartment of service in the body helps drive the church to the actualization of this task. We know very well that, the offices within the church emerge as the result of the need that the local congregation passes through. Therefore, the *enthos* and plagiary of ideas need to be communicated evenly to every member; until they come to the maturity of faith and their perfection of the saint, in their respective function and ministry. As long as each believer is given a place to function, it is very necessary for them to know what the earnest expectation of the office is; even those that are yet to be given a position. The awareness could help them to see what they can contribute to the effective growth of the ministry.

Placement into office

The unhealthy attitude of leadership function that is found in our respective worship center is mostly caused by indiscernible act of placement into office. We commissioned people (workers) into duty (office), without finding out if the individual does have the natural talent and the spiritual gift to offer the service fruitfully. It's like putting square pegs in round holes. We should be reminded that the kingdom of God is concerned with fruitful result. *'You did not choose me, but I chose you and appointed you that you should go and bear fruit and that your fruit should abide, so that whatever you ask the Father in my name, he may give it to you.'* John 15:16. (ESV)

The functions of an office should be understood by the headship. Every office in the body of Christ work towards *'the unity of faith, and the knowledge of the Son of God into a perfect man; unto the measure of the stature of the fullness of Christ'*. Therefore, the act of entrusting an office into one's hand should become more delicate and sensitive. I would say it requires grace to assess the total man and to know his physical capacity (talent) and spiritual capacity (gift).

Some people could be nice as an individual, but that does not justify his capacity to perform up to the set goal. Each office within the local congregation has respective set goal;

walking together to actualize the vision and the mission of the congregation. So, the essence of the office is about the mission of the church and not the 'people'. I wish to clarify this point; the assembly of people of God is the embodiment of God's kingdom. Their mission is to make known the kingdom and walk in the kingdom ethics, but there are necessities that require the kingdom heir to serve; I may call it the 'exercise of love' in the house. The issue of this 'exercise of love' is about the people, but the mission is about God. For the people to discharge these functions, they must have both physical and spiritual capacity.

In a case that one has the spiritual capacity, I will advise; the person's capacity should be examined. If it requires developing the embedded physical capacity in him, then, the church should provide a competent training center for such case. At the other hand if there are no such potentials, I will suggest, the person should be relocated into another office, where he can be worked upon. To every man there are diverse capacities both physical and spiritual. Until the church come to this awareness and start working consciously, they will not make any success on it.

As long as the church has structure and policies; there must be execution of these policies. The desired goal of the church certainly must be met. We should bear in mind we have the task to fulfill we are to make the people become Disciples of Christ. They are to become the instrument of Christ, doing the work of the ministry, and building or equipping others to be like them. So, the work of placing people into office is far different when compared to what most brethren have taken it to be.

The major setback in today's ministry is as a result of this negligence. I desire that all church workers should come to this warning. That wrong placement of people in office without the effective discernment of their measure of faith will become the route to crises. When right persons are place at right position to function, then the vision and burden of the church will be well understood and delivered.

Placement by Personal Interest and Fear of Losing Membership

Giving people office or appointment as a result of personal interest or fear of losing the person's membership certainly will result into ineffectiveness in the discharge of duty. It can further generate other killing disease in administration. To everyone that is in the office as a result of familiarity gain from the pastor(s) will possibly involve in eye-service, overlapping or gapping. As long as these leadership killer diseases exist in the church; the local assembly will suffer set back in their growth.

Furthermore, accredited policy to examine the true conversion and declaration of membership to the local church is very essential; because, if one that is in position is never willing to give his or her commitment as a result of not being satisfied with what is obtainable in the place, the person is subject to gain criticism, fault finding, laying blames, ridiculing and stirring up strife. And we all know that whenever such attitudes grow among members, mostly in the unit ministries, the setting and chaos situation will surely affect the spiritual attainment of the church. Such fruits are the work of the flesh and not the Spirit. Galatians 5:16-17:

'This I say then, Walk in the Spirit, and ye shall not fulfill the lust of the flesh. For the flesh lusteth against the Spirit, and the Spirit against the flesh: and these are

contrary the one to the other: so that ye cannot do the things that ye would.'

Title and Position in Place of Purpose

Crises are bound to grow in any local assembly when the desire for leadership is to gain title and position. Myles Munroe said in his book, 'Becoming a leader'; *"A Title and positioning do not guarantee performance and productivity."* We are in the era where fame becomes the climate of success and achievement and not impact and legacy. Because the people who carnally seek for recognition do all they can to gain position without having the knowledge of the office and its function in the church. As earlier discussed, office exists in any local assembly as a result of needs that arise in the local assembly; therefore, the leaders in position should be functioning with the mind to meet up the needs. They should give their virtues to the perfection of the work of the ministry. But in a situation where the reverse is the case, the local church is expected to face jealousy, prejudice and probably hatred among workers and members. Training the people before calling them into office will help reduce the influence of this attitude.

Headship Influence

It is obvious that many workers in local congregation have genuine zeal for the expansion of the kingdom. But greater percentage of these people has been silenced over basic things that would have helped them grow fast and vast in the work that they are given.

Most head of churches or leadership made themselves the standard and final authority in the kingdom. To them it is what they want the subject to know and do is what is right and not biblical standard that should been given to God's people in God's kingdom. The insecurity of the headship becomes a setback and deters the strength and zeal of the subject.

To this cause, it gives much room to further disunity in the body of Christ. How that anyone that happens to know how low and behind he is in the things of God despite of all his effort to the service of God in his congregation tense to breakout for the safety of his faith. Most head leaders are not concerned about given them the right understanding in the work of the ministry rather, they see the emerging talent and gift in their local congregation as threat to their effort. This in turn gives rise to unnecessary suspicion. Let me put it this way. Any time you feel insecure in your ministry as head of the local congregation, it is an indication that you are not doing your leading God's way. Talent will be discovered always as long as you have members in the church. God is raising these ones for His purpose and plan and no man can stop it.

Respect for Leadership

Since leadership has to do with two or group of persons the leaders in any unit of service in the local church should be able to develop a trusting relationship with others. Seeing the born-again brother as members of the same body; set up confidence above tribal sentiment. *'For just as the body is one and has many members, and all the members of the body; though many, are one body, so it is with Christ. For in one Spirit we were all baptized into one body – Jews or Greeks, slaves or free – and all were made to drink of one Spirit.' 1corinthians 12:12-13. (ESV).* Learn to accept another with love and sincerity. *'Beloved, let us love one another, for love is from God, and whoever loves has been born of God and knows God.' 1John 4:7. (ESV).* But if this is not followed the local church will suffer chaos. Workers weaknesses that would have been corrected and be forgiven will become stigma in the worker's integrity and personality. This can later demoralize his effort towards effective service. The very person has positive values in him. And whenever his weakness is more considered then his positive values will no longer be seen.

We should not forget that coming together is to help one another become what God wants us to be. No man is perfect but by the using of our individual gifts will help bring us into the fullness and the status of Christ. Do not forget *'iron'*, Proverbs 27: 17 says, *'sharpens iron, so a man sharpens the countenance of his friend'*. (NKJV).

The neglect of Worker's Value

Each worker in the local church has a great value and is very important to the local church. His value is of great effect to the growth of the ministry. If he is neglected indirectly, we will be neglecting a section of growth in the local church. But the local church worker if given little acknowledgement and is exposed to more knowledge of his office and calling, will put his very abilities and spiritual gifts into maximum use.

Let us take a look on Romans 12:4, 6:
"For as we have many members in one body, but all the members do not have the same function… "Having then gifts differing according to the grace that is given to us, let us use them…" (NKJV)

To every man is given one or more than one gift. Each one is given in accordance with purpose to function. And grace is given with the gift. Therefore, the man that receives or is called in to an office has grace to manifest the importance of his call. For this purpose, such has to be esteemed with regards. We should not think that we are more important than others.
"For I say, through the grace given to me, to everyone who is among you, not to think of

himself more highly than he ought to think, but to think soberly, as God has dealt to each one a measure of faith." Romans 12:3 (NKJV)

"Let nothing be done through selfish ambition or conceit, but in lowliness of mind let each esteem others better than himself…

"Let each of you look out not only for his own interests, but also for the interests of others." Philippians 2: 3, 4. (NKJV).

Poor communication of vision

Effective communication is a tool that creates room for growth. Whenever people interact with one another, they exchange their values. They create reciprocal atmosphere for ideas, beliefs, passion and strength. These become their protective wall for the purpose that unites them. Church leader must allow this experience to dominate the church. The headship should know that each person in the local church has what is required to handle or control any ministry. They are the essentials of the congregation.

The effective of these persons lie on how the headship presents or communicate his vision and value with the church workers and members. He should guard against unwanted gap in communication. Instruction should be well managed among the church workers. They are the eyes and the bulletin of the members on administrative issues.

The headship and other workers within the local church should build a 'good speaking attitude' as well as 'good listening attitude'. I personally believe leadership is relationship. So, I encourage you to grow this relationship with love and your ministry will be void of chaos and plateau.

Lack of good Listening culture

Should there be good relationship among the people you lead then cultivate the habit to listen more than how you speak. When you constantly give out without receiving you will soon go out of store. Feedback is very necessary for growth and firmness. The people you are leading are very important. They are the very purpose you become the head – leader. Whatever you exercise or you are doing in the ministry is people effectiveness or usefulness in the kingdom to the glory of God. Therefore, the people you are leading have some value that will encourage the continuity of your vision. Giving attention to their response will help you avoid silly mistake that robs the good effort of your passion. You need them to support the growth; but when you are not learning to listen to the people you are leading, then, you are about to creating division among them. This is because some people are very loyal to a fault, they never contribute; while some are good critic and always go after detail explanation for any change. When they are not considered then you are creating room for division and probably disloyalty.

Performance Evaluation Code

Performance Evaluation Code (PEC) should be designed in the local church to help individual workers in the local assembly to evaluate his performance systematically. It is often difficult for self to admit his fault. Pride often crown failure and setback.

*"Pride goeth before destruction, and a haughty spirit before a fall."*Proverbs 16: 18

Let this be known, if you will not consider it necessary to allow yourself to be checked on scale of integrity and performance, you will certainly, gradually lose the drive for kingdom purpose.

"And every man that striveth for the mastery is temperate in all things…" 1Corinthians 9:25.

You have to see it that without evaluation of our input in various areas of commitment; we will end-up be losing the focus unknowingly. It can create room for workers to gap in their function. It will not give room for motivation. And self will grow, leading to pride, jealousy, envy, and others sort of freshly desire.

Please, note the performance report is to help the workers see needs for his change or improve to meet up the evolution of the society. It further helps the workers to remain focus and to meet up the target set for the season by the ministry. If the ministry is your personal ministry, I will suggest that you get other ministers you can trust to help evaluate your performance in your ministry. Sometimes, you take courage; humble yourself before your executive body for either secret or open evaluation. All these exercises are to help you become successful.

Financial influence (Mormonism)

God called us into service. And we are called according to God's purpose and plan. The standard through which each one of us (Christian) comes to God remains unchanged. Therefore, the parameter which we are required to be effective and useful never change. When the church leader or senior pastor or church council, uses financial strength of individuals as requirement for the calling into sacred positions of the church is sincerely going to reap the fruit influence by mormon (money).

"He that trusteth in his riches shall fall…" Proverbs 11:28.

Baby-hood office holder.

This is a state in which the baby in

faith is given sensitive office that should have been given to mature in faith and experienced in ministerial function to hold. The church function is not to be manned by secular professionals. It should be performed by the leading of the Holy Spirit; handled by those that have submitted themselves to the governance of the Holy Spirit. When an office is given to a baby-Christian in faith, the local assembly should equally be prepared to experience spiritual childish decisions and operations.

"He must not be new convert, or he may [develop a beclouded and stupid state of mind] as the result of pride [be blinded by conceit, and] fall into the condemnation that the devil [once] did." 1Timothy 3: 6. (AMP)

It is only in an atmosphere where there are foundational teachings; and basic rules for discipleship is cultivated, then, we can be assured of possible growth that can generate fruitful result. In other word, baby in faith should not be given sensitive office, as these offices are practically given to fulfill God's purpose and not man.

The neglect of character stability

Although growing churches suffer the lack of workers to fill in the emerging offices; it does not mean that the headship should neglect the place of 'attitude of workers. When people whose characters are questionable are given position to occupy, you have set up a table of bad repute on the congregation. And this can in turn affect your headship. You may be called or taken after the manner of your workers.

Most of these attitudes promote crises that can lead to closing down of the local assembly. It is advisable not to give appointment to those who are found wanting in areas such as:

1. Sexual immoral attitude

2. Financial misappropriation attitude

3. Intolerance attitude and others.

He that is slow to anger is better than the mighty; and he that ruleth his spirit than he that taketh a city. Proverbs 16:32

He that hath no rule over his own spirit is like a city that is broken down, and without walls. Proverbs 25:28

Leader inaccessibility

Churches face a lot of crises without knowing the true source to the problem. Whenever the leader is lacking the ability to be accessed by the people he leads; the people will soon become isolated from the vision and mission of the ministry. While they will be there in some respective meetings of the ministry; their contributions to the success thereof become limited. Their trust or confident to work is not strong enough to give them assurance that they are part of what is going on within the ministry and church. As long as the content of their faith is limited so also, it affects their spiritual fruitfulness. The devil can capitalize on this and create much fruit of the flesh which will lead to disunity among the people.

Conclusively, the inability to identify the source of a problem on its own is an ailment itself. Once a problem is identified, its route cause can be traced or where deviations actually occurred. In solving these problems, one must be realistic to highlight reasons why they were grounded instead of sailing steadily with a view to correcting them. How a man receives correction is yet another problem. The leader who really wants to improve will appreciate and welcome any better approach, constructive criticism.

It is my desire that you will humble yourself and consider few of these things that suffered many churches in this generation setback, both spiritually and physically. We have to build God's church to maturity. This is the reason we are called.

MAKE YOUR NOTE

CHAPTER FOUR

Close observation in the modern church era proves that the church although is spreading wide and large in sizes does not grow inwardly. The church is becoming the state of social gathering. Some ecclesiastic analysts say it is the center of alternative of material wants. This is a leading issue to this present generation. Leaders in the church are left to ask themselves, what impact are we making in the church?

Today Discipleship is a standard topic for study in churches and groups. Seminars on discipleship abound, and there is no question of the importance of the subject. It is one thing to master the biblical principles of discipleship, but quite another to transfer those principles into everyday life. We are in the church era that the leaders care less over the spiritual health being of the disciples and members. The discipleship culture only becomes college and seminary knowledge and not the church mandate.

The purpose of the church is to make the people the alliance in their citizenship. It will be a gross negligence if we will not spell out what is the deviance in the modern church. The modern church operates with a lot of alternative. It becomes clearer to us when we realize what were the foreseeing challenges awaiting the church of Christ. The challenges that were awaiting the church are the reason why Christ gave gifts to men and the commissioning. The modern church has shifted in focus from the real need in the church and started solving the felt need; and feels complete in it. The real need has to do with those essentials that are required to certify our relationship and the inheritance of promise. The church should be a place to restructure the mindset (attitude) of the people (believers) seeking the kingdom and its treasure first before coming to the perishing things of our mortal living, the felt need. Take note, Jesus said that felt needs are basic necessities that minister to the body and all are liable to destruction.

The real need as elaborated in the scriptures is for building of the church and it was that which the church was founded. We cannot deny the fact on discipleship. It is a task the Master, Jesus committed into our hands as leaders. One of the leadership qualifications we learn from the scripture, is the ability of the leaders to teach; 1Timothy 3:2. Jesus commissioned the New Testament church leaders to make disciples of all nations. This is where we are failing. Churches are struggling to keep the pace of evangelism in their respective local centers. But no one easily realizes that the soul brought into the church needs to be effectively disciplined to Christ-like life. It is unhealthy and distorting if the church will not be able to build up Christ-like followers for the kingdom of God.

Christ Discipleship Philosophy

The earthly ministry of Jesus Christ was not only to reveal the Father to the world and to begin the work of salvation; but he came and made himself an example to us who believe. In John 17:12, he said,

"While I was with them, I protected them and kept them safe by that name you gave me." (NIV).

These imply that Jesus protected and kept the Father's souls (Disciples) by taking them through the pattern of life that pleases the Father. He showed them the standard of God's righteousness. He did not only instruct them but lived the life. The very things He went through, He encouraged them to get ready to pass through the same.

He placed Himself as an example for us to learn how to discipline our emotions till we become perfect before the Father. He gave us the love of the Father. He showed us how to love Him.

"For I have given you an example, that you should do as I have done to you." John13:15. (NKJV)

Christ Discipleship philosophy was a call.

To learn from Him: Jesus wanted us to learn from Him the things He went through. He endued the cross set before Him. At last obtain the crown. *"Looking unto Jesus…who for the joy that was set before Him endured the cross, despising the shame, and has sat down at the right hand of the throne of God."* Hebrews 12:2 (NKJV).

To His disciplined lifestyle: A disciplined lifestyle is what Jesus commended us to live. Having the ability to control our self in chaotic situation. It is the one of the earnest fruits of matured Christian.

To live life in His way of relation with the Father and to others: Christ made himself our example. He lived among men and shared with man what the love of the Father is. Here He commanded, 'love one another'; this will prove we are His followers.

To learn standard of life: In Matthew's gospel, Jesus took His time to elaborate the standard of life in God's kingdom. And this is one of the most challenging standards of life. This is the greatest remark from Jesus to the Church – His disciples – 'You are the salt of the earth…you are the light of the world.' *Read Matthew 5.*

What Discipleship should be considered

Considering the following facts on what

discipleship is it will bring us into a clearer picture of what the negligence has caused the modern church in this part of the world. Therefore,

- Discipleship is not counting heads but the counting of dedicated souls
- Discipleship is development of values in life
- Discipleship is process of synthesis, circumcising and husbandry.

Discipleship is not counting heads but the counting of dedicated souls

This is where most modern churches get it wrong. The numbers of person that come to the church do not become the disciples of the church. To disciple means to discipline other. It means bringing into the fullness of what you personally believe and live for. This means that, you are already a proven disciple of Christ.

Certainly, the mandate the church has is

on discipleship making. Problems will become less and controllable in the church only when the mind-set of the modern leaders is directed towards the perfecting of saints and growing into the unity of faith. But in a situation in which the church is operating on the foundation of numbers than on souls building; it becomes obvious that those that will come in the leadership function will be half-baked Christian (nominal). With this, the church will be facing conflict that may be reducing growing strength of the local congregation. In other words, there has to be a steady growing positive correlation between the growth rate in numbers and the actual disciples that is both quantitative and qualitative.

Balancing these challenges, we have to see church leadership beyond how many sits in the auditorium; how many turns of service in a day we hold but should shift to souls building. We have to come to this acceptance, that the people in the auditorium come so that, you as a leader should disciple them. Raising these people in the standard of the kingdom ethics till they come into maturity and are effectively productive to the body of Christ, this is the mandate. John says, in the fifteen chapters.

"This is to my Father's glory, that you bear much fruit, showing yourselves to be my disciples" verses 8. (NIV)

Discipleship is development of value

The Bible is a complete composition of leadership values. Our Bible studies supposed to be the basic school for all church leaders. More so, the local church Bible study program should be richly developed to cover all areas of life that will help the congregation become more productive. If your congregation as a pastor is not discipleship oriented, you may have much people in attendance but less committed people to your vision. Learning is the essentials of growth. The belief system of your disciples is secured through learning. Therefore, what we learn is what builds our value system. Should the people become what we expect them to be in the congregation, then, what we give to them matters.

Take note of this, whatever vision God gave to you can be best known and understood by its biblical confirmation. There is no God given vision and calling that do not have it bases in the scripture. Therefore, if the congregation is short of biblical precept, they are bound to ignorantly be opposing your success in calling. The more your workers in the church have sound teaching of the Bible and deeper relationship with God, the more the passion to please God become the ultimate priority in service. And this in-turn will reduce the conflict in the departments or unit ministries in the church.

The process of Synthesis, Circumcision,

and Husbandry

"Therefore, go and make disciples of all nations…" Matthew 28:19. (NIV).

The church leaders have to give prior attention to this process. They have to understand that the body of Christ will not be able to grow effectively and crises controllable until they advance in discipleship concept.

To 'make disciples' is the process of transforming one from the common or known to a new form or better quality. The crisis in the church is strongly linked up to the attitude of our discipleship. The making process is what the local church leaders must come to do daily in their church – congregation. You have to build them. Change them from what they were and make them become what God wants them to be. *"To make them holy, cleansing them by the washing with water through the word"* emphasis added, Ephesians 5: 26,

(*TNIV*). It is the word of God that will transform your local congregation to "*a glorious church without a spot or wrinkle or any other blemish. Instead, she will be holy and without fault.*" Ephesians 5:27 (*NLT*).

Your message, program should have a sole purpose to reach the least person in the congregation. You should make them become useful to the kingdom of God.

The members of the church should be considered as one that needs to develop characters that are Christ-like; inculcate value-pattern; and controlling their behavior. These things can only be done successfully only if proper attention is given to the teaching ministry. Giving adequate room that can embrace the difference and obscurity in their life. Don't ever forget, it is your obligation to transfer the baton of this gospel race to the next generation. How will you do it?

Process of Discipleship Making

The following points suggested will help you position your effort to bring the convert to effective disciple and member to your local congregation.

(1)   *Consecration unto greater commitment*

Separation or disengagement from any form of distraction and total submission should be the dying word of the disciple. The person intending to become a disciple must consecrate himself and give up worldly values. Separation from the entanglement of the world should be a matter of priority to the disciple. He should emulate deep consecration of his masters' vision and mission, who does not want distraction and interference to disrupt what he wants to achieve. For instance, Jesus knew his vision and mission, so he upheld a deep consecration that the disciples in turn emulated.

"Therefore, if anyone cleanses himself from what is dishonorable, he will be a vessel for honorable use, set apart as holy, useful to the master of the house, ready for every good work. So, flee youthful passions and pursue righteousness, faith, love, and peace, along with those who call on the Lord from pure heart." 2Timothy 2: 21-22. ESV.

When a disciple becomes deeply consecrated, having separated himself from the masses, the possibility of greater commitment becomes a reality. He becomes serious in business, concerns himself with principles and strategies on how to carry on the vision and the mission to please the master. Take note, the scripture says, *'pursue'* your dedication to your God; try hard to keep up rightness, faith, love and peace at all time with those – people of same belief – wherever they are found. Be always ready to keep up whatever that will bring you down from this great honor the Father through Christ have given to us.

(2) *Sharing of vision and participation*

It is of necessity that sharing of vision should be of immense significance in discipleship making. The leader has the sole responsibility to make known his vision and mission to his disciples. Proper sharing of vision is a strong tool for a successful mission accomplishment. Whatever the area of the leader's ministerial concentration could be should share with his disciples for understanding.

The disciples in this respect have the sole responsibility to participate and get seriously involved in the accomplishment of the vision through useful suggestions and contributions. The disciple participating does not work in new ideas independent of the master's vision, rather in loyalty goes ahead to fulfill his obligations.

In the process of involvement, the disciples should be allowed to use their different gifts and abilities to enhance the speedy fulfillment of the vision and mission. Deprivation from the use of gifts and abilities might deter the speed at which the vision is fulfilled. The disciple involved should not use such gifts and talent for self-glory.

(3) *Training and building of the disciples*

Jesus called the twelve disciples; he brought them under his training process that they might develop the basic skills needed for the actualization of his vision and mission. Do not assume that the persons called into the work of the ministry have the ability to function at the best-required standards. It is true that everyone has received a measure of gift and talents from the Lord, but they are to be properly developed especially in the light of a contemporary society. Times and trends are never the same from generation to generation; they must be built to work in the suitability of the time for harmony.

(4)   *Supervision and reinforcement of skills for greater achievement*

Practical participation in the communication of the vision requires certain skills. The disciple, after his theoretical is not an expert. He needs practical application of the vision. In this regard, it is necessary that the disciple falls back to base for supervision of work done and possible reinforcement where difficulty was met. The idea of giving up is never a slogan in the process of making disciples. The sense of defeat is not a fact of concern for a heart caught and full of vision. Success is always the focus that makes reinforcement a reality for greater achievements.

Embedded in the discipleship is the emphasis and faith on the rewards of true discipleship, loyalty, powers and winning the confidence of the Holy Spirit. It also includes the cleansing and purification of the mind, body and soul awaiting the habitation of Christ. It must be clarified that the denial of these worldly lust paves way for spiritual growth. Once a worker is convinced about this, he will voluntarily give his best.

Bad leadership examples also

contaminate the confidence of growing disciples. The luxurious lifestyle of pastors seems to negate the belief in denial of worldly things. Since your action speaks louder than your preaching; you have to live life that exemplifies what you believe. Your workers looked up to you for their choice. You are their spiritual father. They believe you are guaranteed to make heaven therefore, whatever you do seems to be right.

The reward of servanthood is great. The disciple should not allow sentiment and other factors stop him from achieving greater things for God and, as well as driving himself for greater rewards. It is twofold – Material rewards and Eternal rewards- for agreeing to be a disciple and a disciple indeed. Crowns await every true and successful disciple in heaven. If you are a faithful and good servant, you shall be welcomed into the abundance of your Father right here and hereafter. Be a disciple with totality of heart.

"And, behold, I come quickly; and my reward is with me, to give every man according as his work shall be." Rev 22:12

MAKE YOUR NOTE

CHAPTER FIVE

The term 'church membership' is often argued by some people, as not been biblical term. There is no dispute about that; yet we can't neglect the fact that the assembly of brethren is as a result of a given purpose and belief. People have come to share the same understanding of their faith. Since the local church has to do with people that has mutual acceptance in goal and vision; the term 'membership' become most preferable to define the acceptance of purpose and belief.

So, when we talk about local church membership, we are referring to the gathering of the saints. But it is difficult to say, the modern church is made up of the saints. The reason is that, most of the said members within a given denomination is crowded with people that do not know if they are *Regenerated* (*Born-again*); do not know, what is the difference between the '*testimony of salvation*' of the soul and the '*testimony of compassion*' toward bodily needs. It also, becomes a common mistake that when someone is in the church for sometimes, he is regarded as a member in the church. In trying to view this comment, it does lead people to ask, who are the members of a church?

What is membership?

To be a member in any body (it can be a church, club or association), the person must be willing to.

1. Accept the existence or operation of the body.
2. He should have the readiness to abide by the rules and regulations of the body, and
3. Dutifully, accept whatever charge is laid upon him, also, to
4. Keep the reputation of the mutuality.
5. Accept the vision of the local church.
6. Be committed and passionately serve to the accomplishment of any goal set by the local church.

However, a Christian is a member of the

church of Christ. That is, the church consists of the people of God that are built together into spiritual building for God's habitation. Ephesians 2:20-22.

'And (Christians) *are built upon the foundation of the apostles and prophets, Jesus Christ himself being the chief corner stone; In whom all the building fitly framed together groweth unto an holy temple in the Lord: In whom ye also are builded together for an habitation of God through the Spirit.'* Emphasis added.

Membership is simply the identical nature of oneness of persons with mutuality of common belief. We are important in the church of Christ. Our membership must be valued. It should be allowed to bring joy to others: to encourage and build the unity of life to the glory of God. We will look at it as; coming together is to help one another become what God wants us to be.

What is not Membership?

Several cultures are brought into church of God. And cultures have been misrepresented as standard through which membership is confirmed. We have to accept the biblical truth as the standard for confirming the rightness of any things we do in our local church.

Firstly, the local church is the composition of people. Secondly, these persons are God's people and do not belong to any pastor or church founder. Thirdly, God gave us his people for us (ministers) to shepherd them. Fourthly, whatever is pleasing in the sight of God should be what the shepherd should set-forth to the members of the local-church.

In this regard, what is often regarded as criteria for membership such as tithing, payment of dues, silly rules and handshakes, buying of membership attendance card, performance of meaningless rituals, do not transform attendant into membership. In chapter one, the composition of the church was discussed. And this should be what every leader in the body of Christ should embrace. We are not gathering our people, but they are God's people. We did not convict them, but that was done by the Holy Spirit. We only see them coming to God and not us. They heard the message of God through us and not our message through God. Therefore, we have this obligation and we must be committed to it; to incorporate the people of God in the local church which is a unit of God's family by biblical principles.

Those who are willing to join the family of God with you should know.

1. What the Family (the local church) is all about?

2. What purposes gave birth to the

family?

3. What will be the benefit through this family unit?

4. What is the family structure of operation?

5. If they are qualified for this?

6. If they join what shall be their responsibility?

7. Is there a place if they chose to join?

8. How will they start their membership function?

Who is a member?

Practically, the congregation we have is born-out of community. The community is the environment we locate our worship center. These ones were unchurched later become attendants to our programs organized in our local church. At this state, it will be misnomer to place in position someone who have not come to full knowledge and understanding of the local congregation. Since membership is about commitment to the service and growth of a particular local assembly. In this regard, the local assembly should balance their confession over attendance and membership.

A member should be regarded as one who has come to the point of conviction in faith and willfully accept the membership covenant of the assembly; and firmly share mutually in the vision and love of the local assembly.

Many will certainly come to program that you run in the local church, even some will regularly be present in the activities of the church; the fact is that, at such point they are only available and not committed to the vision and love of the church.

'As ye have therefore received Christ Jesus the Lord, so walk ye in him: Rooted and built up in him, and established in the faith, as ye

have been taught, abounding therein with thanksgiving.' Colossians 2: 6, 7.

Why Attendance?

'*…And the Lord added to the Church daily such as should be saved…..'* Acts 2:47.

In every Church program termed successful is primarily measured first on the number of attendance then effect or impact created in the life of the attendance. There is something you should examine here. The Lord brings the people to hear the message He had given the church. Secondly, some people heard and believe the message. Thirdly, they are at your disposal. The question is what will you do with them?

If the leaders in the church keep watching them coming every service, it does not signify that you are actually fruitful. They are only available for you to birth them with the local assembly DNA. If they are not inculcated; I mean unattended to, to nurture them to the maturity of faith, it should be guaranteed that whatever they came with from the community will soon become their 'breed' identity while in the church.

When the baby-convert is given a position to function in the church as result of been available, then the ministry should be prepared to face negative crises (the working of the flesh).

Therefore, the attendance is given by God that you should turn them into members. Breeding them with the 'brand of the ministry: Ensuring the safety of their faith and destiny. Never de-valuing their personality; give them sense of love; appreciating their availability and sense of belonging. Design a forum that can build them up with the culture of faith within the local church.

Membership Class

The church is a place where souls are modified into the pattern of God's concept. Therefore, membership class is a pre-discipleship class which embraces and addresses things that are observed by the church seekers (those who are not members of the local church but have started worshiping in the congregation with interest to continue).

Membership class is the first training session given to those who are willing to be part of what is happening in the local church. In this regard, the class should be designed to give attention to things that made-up the local congregation. Leaders of local church should know this; as local church, it is composed of different persons. And these persons are coming together to form a unique body which is part of the universal church. The individual persons are coming into oneness of the vision and purpose of the local congregation. It is only in the membership class that serves as orientation or induction stage for all incoming believers. That can be used to competently incorporate them into the beauty of the local congregation.

Safety to membership

Much safety is guaranteed in your ministry when your attendants are turned into members. The standard for membership gives more or firm confident on success of your church vision and mission.

This is essential; those who have the understanding on what it takes to become members in the local church will know that the success of their membership is reciprocal to the success and effectiveness of the church. But where your ministry do not have a functional guide or biblical standard for membership; as the attendants come from community and are given privileged without 'circumcising' them from community skin; the church is bound to be run in the flesh. In such situation, the fruit of the flesh is going to grow and dominate the church.

Do not forget, you are running God's business. Therefore, you need God's wisdom to effectively manage it. What is your membership structure? Are they biblically canonized?

The Commissioning

Understanding the purpose of the church will be of great help to shape the focal vision of the church. What I mean is that, when the leadership and the church know the reason why the local gathering was found and their functions. Therefore, they will be able to bring all things within their reach under control.

The membership of the local church will be sharpened and be controlled by the purpose. At this point old members and the new member will have the same sense of commitment to accomplish their ministries inter-dependently without creating destructive environment. Each one will find it a pleasure to help any believer around him to discover his abilities and spiritual gifts. This will give encouragement to the success of one other.

The commissioning is completed when the new convert comes to relationship with God and is become fruitful in the kingdom. That is, the member becomes a lay minister in the local congregation. The lay minister at this point is able to define his ministry and can set up goals that will further the growth of the local church. He can also reproduce his kind in the local assembly from the winning of the soul, and the making of the soul to become a lay minister. This is wonderful!

MAKE YOUR NOTE

CHAPTER SIX

THE TEACHING INDUSTRY IN CHURCHES

Most church leaderships are yet to cultivate the teaching habit. This is the sector that builds and strengthens the growth of membership. The challenges the churches are undergoing can be reduced only when church leaders make up to teach everyone the rudiment of citizenship in Christ. When the church leaders start working on individual life, confronting their sinning habit and discipline administered; then, the church will regain the authority to establish dominion in the earth, and righteousness will flourish fruitfully wherever it is gathered

The biblical qualifications of our church leaders are rich enough to make them competent teachers of the faith in Christ. It is required that churches should ensure that all workers have the ability to influence the members of the local church through their respective offices.

The ultimate aim of bringing one into assembly is to make one become like us in Christ; bringing the people together, to see, know and do all things in the same way. By this process, the church is to change from glory to glory in every day of fellowship and her life.

"And they continued steadfastly in the apostles' doctrine and fellowship, and in breaking of bread, and in prayers. And all that believed were together, and had all things common; And they, continuing daily with one accord in the temple, and breaking bread from house to house, did eat their meat with gladness and singleness of heart." Acts 2:42, 44, 46

Why teaching industry?

The church must not forget the ultimate purpose of the kingdom as Christ reveals. I often see the Church as a body designed by the Father to culture His Children. Whenever a soul is added to the church, it is done that soul should be transformed to the conformity of the real image of sonship. The Bible helps us to know that Christ Jesus is the true example of our sonship. In the gospel John, He declares himself as the only way to the Father. Meaning, whatever links us to God must be tested and acceptable in Christ Jesus. As it is clearly known, the church is the body of Christ. What Jesus is, is what the Church should be.

Jesus said, those who accepted him by the preaching of the gospel should be taught the kingdom principle as God in Christ wants us to share in the glory He has. He wants the church to be the continuous radiant of His image and glory. These people are gathered in the name of Jesus unto God. They should be led into the experience of the fellowship of the glorious body.

Role Models

Becoming a worker in the church is likewise becoming the role model in the church. Since leadership is character and not profession, workers in the local church should know that it is an opportunity to give himself for the effective transformation of his heart and head for the service.

The position is given not for self-aggrandizement but as privilege to serve. In other words, it is an opportunity given to influence souls for the kingdom. It is a privilege to contribute or increase the fruit of the kingdom. Therefore, a humble spirit is required for successful performance. Whatever we sow in the people we serve is what guarantees what kind of fruit they will produce for the kingdom.

Furthermore, until workers in the church see themselves as servants and choose to humble themselves to watch and care over the flock of the LORD, it will be accounted unto them as unfruitful servant. For this reason, earnest discipline is demanding on us in order for us to give out what the LORD our Master gives us to minister.

More so, we are to attract people to the kingdom. To show the people the true manner of life as the Master taught. Jesus in one of His greatest sermons declares that we are the light of the world. In this concept, he was proclaiming to the church that knowledge and standard of life lies in the hand of the children of the kingdom. We are to show the world the knowledge of Truth and life; what God the Creator has made and the purpose of the life He gave. Therefore, every appointed worker or leader in the church has many responsibilities first, with himself; and secondly, with the people he is leading. If a leader or worker lives the purpose-life, the mission statement of the local church will become their role mode. If this becomes the personality for all workers in the church, this will produce a positive result within the members.

Action speaks louder than word

Let us examine the following points and set up our ministry into legacy.

The church workers always have the privilege of investing his life into the lives of others.

Examining the effect of impact on small group, it is evidential that the best format to influence people for change is in small unit. Every leader has this opportunity to inculcate the truth of faith and life-pattern into the members of the local congregation.

He must recognize that his words and actions are influencing others to bring tremendous responsibility as well as honor.

The more people in the small unit of the ministry get to know the purpose, vision and the entire church. It becomes more commitment to the people to discharge the set duty that is before them. Getting people to do the right thing in the house of God and staying away from thing that brings chaos and disunity is that, each leader should cultivate the habit of passing right information in the right way and at right time to the people. Helping them to know reasons behind each decision made by the church council as understanding is one of the strengths of unity and commitment in any organization.

He must be committed to set a pace for the disciples.

The congregation sees you as a personality that is worth emulating. It stands as a demand that you have to put daily evaluation on your everyday exercise. Your personal life and that in the ministry has no difference. Because you have a Father who sits in Heaven and knows all that you do both in secret and in public.

"For to this you were called, because Christ also suffered for us, leaving us example, that you should follow His steps:" 1Peter 2: 21.

Discipleship of Church Workers

Church workers are people set aside for specific function in the local assembly. They ensure the orderliness of the operation of the service and other essential needs of the local church.

The church workers are priests in God's kingdom. It is exponential that all priests are to be equipped with knowledge of God's Word. The Priest of God is designated to minister God's ordinance to God's people. It is clearer from Malachi 2:7; 'For the priest's lips should keep knowledge…' The priest is the first preserve library of God's kind of knowledge in the kingdom.

Followers (disciples in the congregation) learn more by observation. They are convinced very easily when their leaders show more of the scripture in their action. It will be advisable that:

a. ***The pastor should recruit training scheme for workers in his local congregation.*** Workers that are well trained do have confidence in themselves. More so, because they have the knowledge of what they are called to do. It is very ideal for them to put efficiency to every committed task.

b. ***The pastor should introduce workers Bible study.*** Bible study scheme should have a good learning plan. Good successes lie in the experience and well plan discipleship. What they have as bread of life is what they will share with others in the same congregation and outside.

c. ***Ministerial techniques should be shared with the workers.*** If the church workers know what the cost, they have to pay in ministry; they will become better instrument that will give great support to your vision. In other word, they invest their resources - financial, material, natural and spiritual abilities - towards the success of the vision.

d. ***The belief of the local congregation and the doctrine should be taught in detail, first to the workers before the general congregation.*** It is the right of the workers and members of the church to know the rule of conduct and belief as touching the local assembly and the tenet of faith as touching the Christian foundation of faith.

e. ***The pastor should introduce his prayer life scheme to the workers.*** When the church workers become prayer oriented as their headship, effective force is developed; this silence every tendency that will have affected the anticipated growth of the church. More so, in their respective departments or ministries, the same praying life will be seen to be transferred into the members of that unit.

Discipleship of Members

The reason for the gathering of the church is for the effective working of the ministry, the perfecting of the saint and the edifying of the church, which is the body of Christ. In this regards the worker should know the chances they have toward disciples; and the pastors taken advantage to reduce ignorance among the members of his local gathering.

a. Informed church worker is personally qualified to independently disciple members within the church and outside the church.

b. Many times, new converts depend on the workers in the church to update his knowledge about the place of his worship.

c. Members in the congregation show more appreciation to the entire church when workers of the church cover much for their spiritual growth.

d. Workers in the church can fortify the unity. If they become the disciple makers.

e. The workers in the church shape the members through their experience shared.

f. Informed workers are good instruments that spot out the need that requires attention within the church.

g. The workers with vision and mission of the local church easily influence the congregational members with it.

h. The spiritual life of the head pastor can easily be communicated through the church worker.

i. Workers who are mature serve as immediate emergence counselor and advocate to develop issues in the absence of or not easily reach head-pastor.

MAKE YOUR NOTE

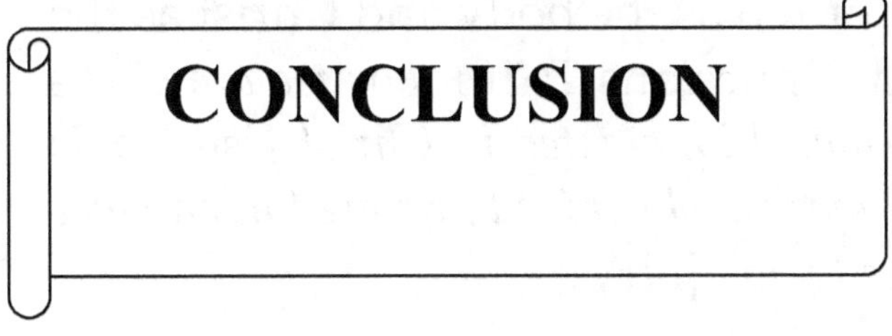
CONCLUSION

The followings are essentials that will enhance pastors and church workers to bring crises in the church under effective control if they will be put into remembrance.

Any office in the church is born as the result of need that the growing church embraces. It is required of the worker to give out adequately to the expectancy of the church as the body and Christ as the head. Ephesians 2: 10; *'For we are God's workmanship, created in Christ Jesus to do good works, which God prepared in advance for us to do.'* [NIV]

The office occupied in the body of Christ is not about power, position or title; it is all about Jesus Christ and what he wants. The unbelievers see position as place to exercise power and oppression over the people. They ascribed to themselves titles and prefix it to their name. To some it is emblem of achievement. Ephesians 4:17; *'So I tell you this, and insist on it in the Lord, that you must no longer live as the Gentiles do, in the futility of their of their thinking'*. (NIV)

The exercise of duty should be in the name of the Lord and to the glory of God; and not that we might be recognized and appreciated by man. 2Corinthians 10: 17; *'However, let him who boast, and glories boast and glory in the LORD'*. (AMP).

Spirit filled church worker can only have a passion for the work that is within the church and always desire for the growth and achievement of others in the area of commitment. 2 Timothy 2: 24; *'And the servant of the Lord must not strive; but be gentle unto all men, apt to teach, patient'*.

He can hereby have the ability to orient, involve and equip other workers and members of the local church. 1Corinthians 10:23,24; *'"Everything is permissible"- but not everything is beneficial. "Everything is permissible" – but not everything is constructive. Nobody should seek his own good, but the good of others.'* [NIV]

Discipleship is the effective way we can consolidate the ministry in our hand. Each worker has the task of helping others realize their gifts, making the experiences the reality of their salvation in Christ Jesus. It will be needful to bring to attention: the church is the 'body of disciples' and 'church goers', therefore, it is the place of the pastors and the workers to ensure that the one within the local congregation is disciplined to be like them. By so doing the local congregation is growing from strength to strength.

But in the situation where the above facts are neglected, the local church, certainly, will become the seat for the flesh to dominate and control the affair of the church in place of the Holy Spirit. If this is the case in your local church, I mean you are seeing more carnality in the church than the Holy Spirit; then, you have to give room for change. Be prepared to accept any shaking the change will produce. The interesting thing is it is working for the good of your service and obedience to God.

'Nevertheless, the foundation of God standeth sure, having this seal, "The Lord knoweth them that are his." 2Timothy 2:19.

MAKE YOUR NOTE

Recommended books

Becoming a Leader; Myles Munroe

The Spirit of Leadership; Myles Munroe

Purpose Driven Church; Rick Warren

Educational Ministry of a Church; Charles A. Tidwell

Rediscovery God's Church; Derek Prince

Growing Strong Churches; Bill Scheidler

Handful of Purpose; W. T. P Wolston

Spiritual Discipleship; J Oswald Sanders

Leading and Managing your Church; Carl F. George and Robert E. Logan

Lead like Jesus; Ken Blanchard and Phil Hodges

Proper attitude toward Leadership; Robyn Gool

THE LITTLE WORM THAT EATS THE APPLE

This is God-given Revelation designed to furnish leaders with the heart to work in the church in God's way.

Practically, it is designed to expose the power of conventional attitude operating within the modern-day church. Drawing their attention to balance most acclaimed 'God said' placement of people in place of responsibility in the local church.

Crucial issues discussed are contemporary challenges in the church in Nigeria and Africa. This book covers areas such as: -

- ❖ The true concept of a Christian and calling.
- The church Leadership concept.
- ❖ The falsified nuggets that corrupt the beauty of church and purpose.

- The feeding process in Christ paradigm
- ❖ The most neglected membership exercise.
- ❖ Affirmative teaching culture for reliable growth.

Samuel Johnson is a conference speaker. He runs Rehoboth Christian Network – A grassroot Leadership development body. Former coordinator Jubilee Bible College, Western campus.

He is married to Ronke Johnson and is blessed with four kids

Little Worms That Eat The Apple – Samuel
Johnson